THE

DEFENCE OF CAWNPORE.

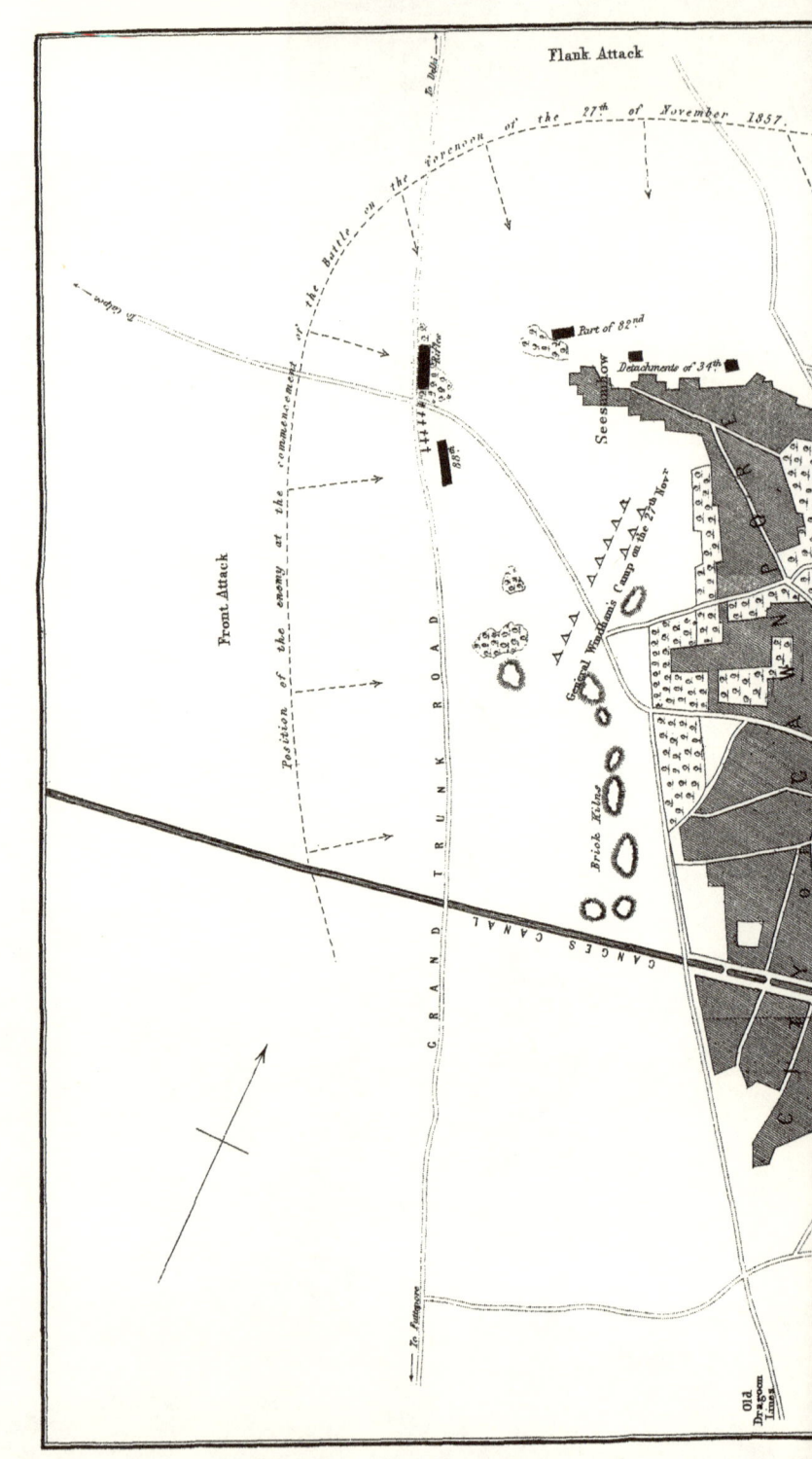

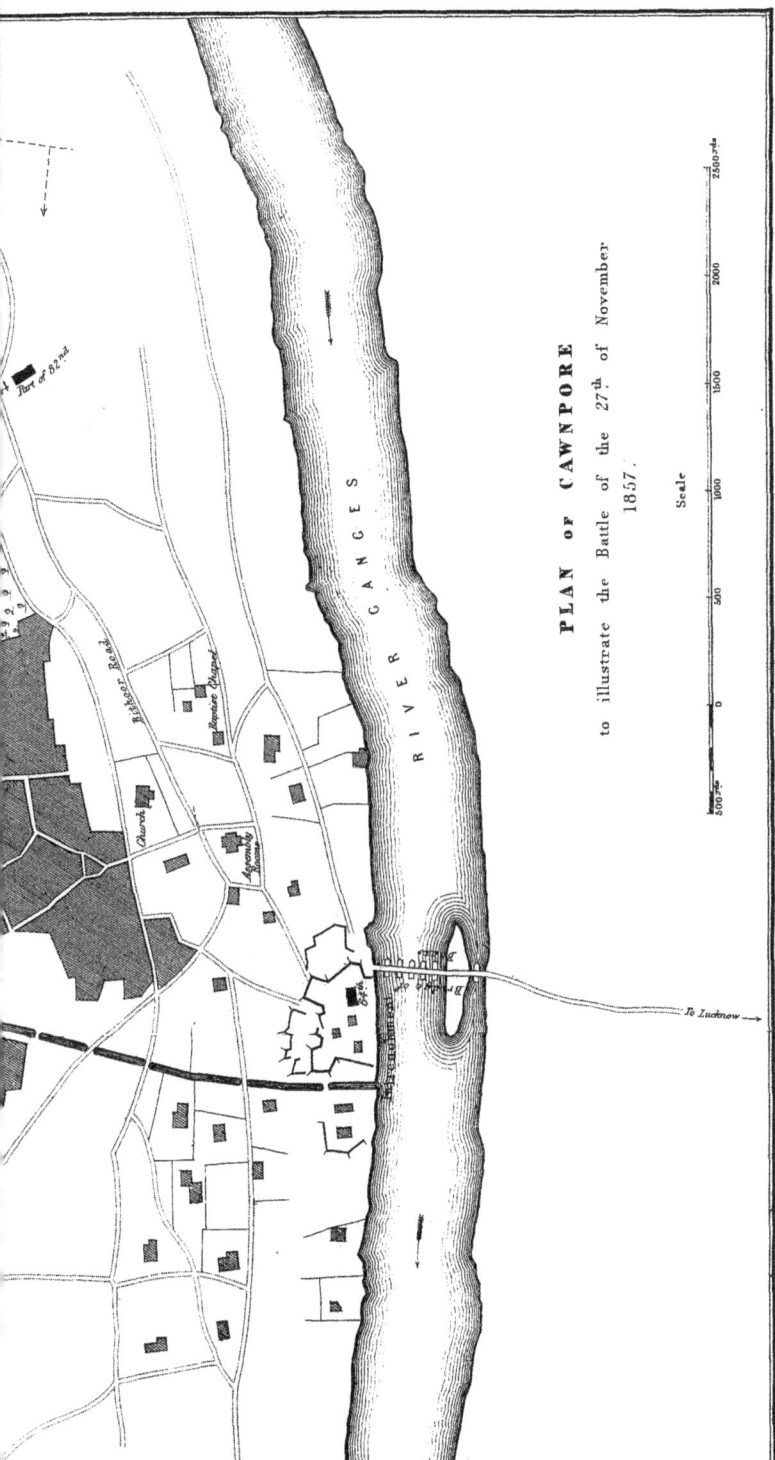

THE
DEFENCE OF CAWNPORE

BY THE TROOPS UNDER THE ORDERS

OF

MAJOR GENERAL CHARLES A. WINDHAM, C.B.

IN NOVEMBER 1857

WRITTEN BY
LIEUTENANT COLONEL JOHN ADYE, C.B.
ROYAL ARTILLERY

The Naval & Military Press Ltd

published in association with

**FIREPOWER
The Royal Artillery Museum**
Woolwich

Published by
The Naval & Military Press Ltd
Unit 10 Ridgewood Industrial Park,
Uckfield, East Sussex,
TN22 5QE England
Tel: +44 (0) 1825 749494
Fax: +44 (0) 1825 765701
www.naval-military-press.com

in association with

FIREPOWER
The Royal Artillery Museum, Woolwich
www.firepower.org.uk

In reprinting in facsimile from the original, any imperfections are inevitably reproduced and the quality may fall short of modern type and cartographic standards.

PREFACE.

In giving an account of the operations before Cawnpore by the troops under Major General Windham, when attacked by the Gwalior Contingent and other mutineers in November, 1857, my object is to endeavour to remove certain erroneous impressions, which appear to have been entertained respecting them.

I imagine these impressions to have arisen from a want of knowledge of details, and I have therefore simply related the circumstances, as they came under my observation.

JOHN ADYE,
Lieut. Col. Royal Artillery.

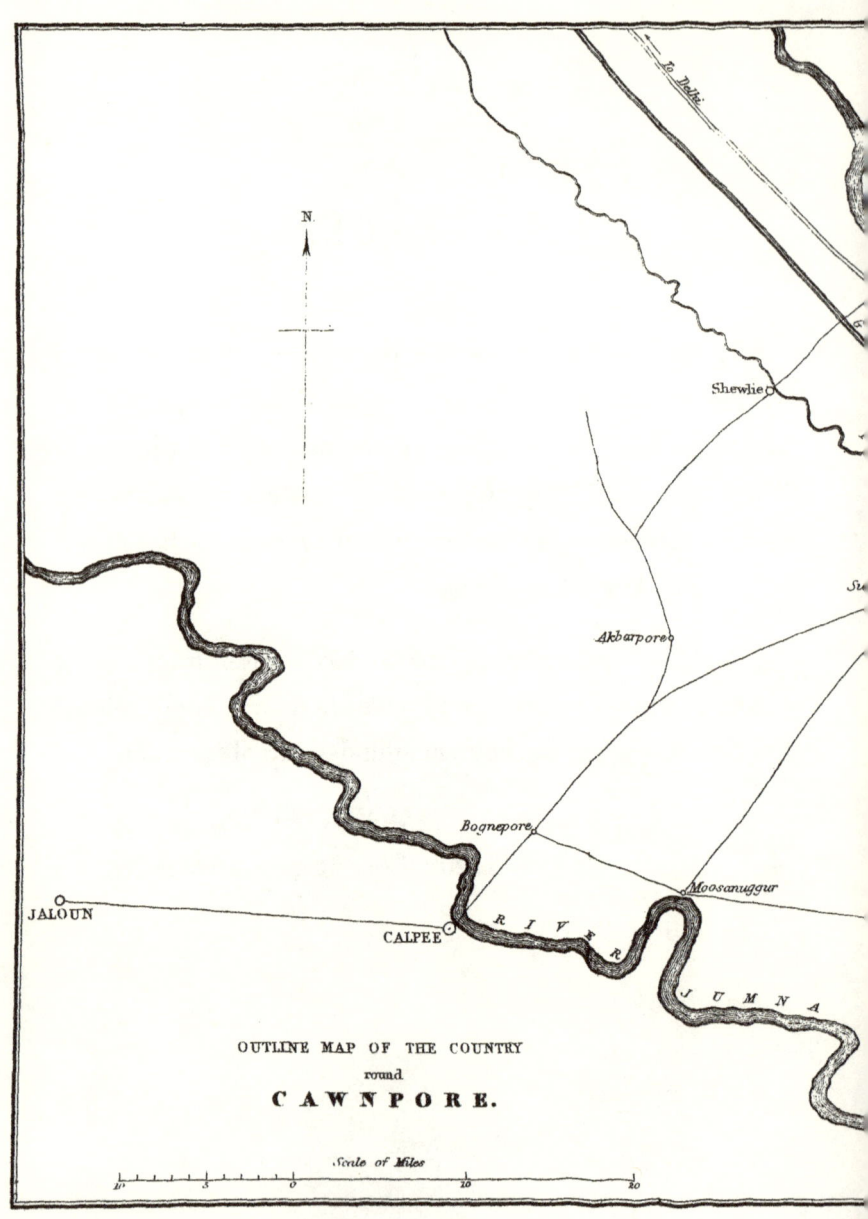

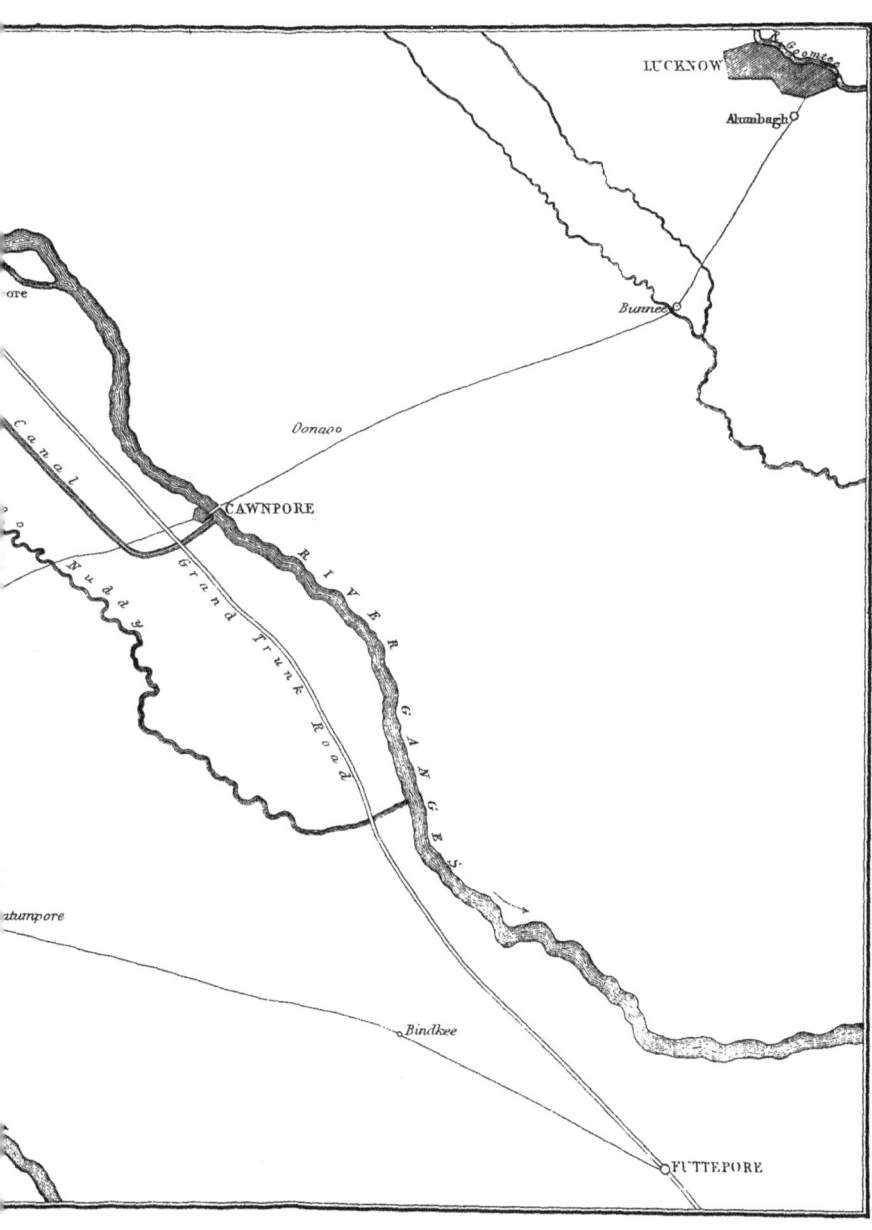

DEFENCE OF CAWNPORE.

CHAPTER I.

Preliminary remarks—The garrison of Lucknow—their critical position in November—Departure of the Commander-in-chief—The garrison of Cawnpore—Description of the intrenchment—its defects—General Windham's instructions—His active measures and preparations—The Gwalior Contingent—their previous inaction—Perilous position of Cawnpore—The Gwalior Contingent cross the Jumna about the middle of November—Detail of their position and numbers—Probability of their attacking Cawnpore—Increased exertions of General Windham—His garrison increased—His constant communications to the chief of the staff at Lucknow—The three courses open to General Windham—1. To attack the enemy in detail—2. To take up a defensive position outside the city of Cawnpore—3. To defend the intrenchment—Details of his views on all these three plans—The advantages and objections considered—The canal scheme—The communications with Lucknow interrupted—General Windham's anxieties increase—His uncertainty as to the safety of the army at Lucknow—The threatening position of the Gwalior Contingent—The post at Bunnee Bridge surprised by the Oude mutineers—A Madras regiment and two guns detached there—Arrival of a note from Lucknow concealed in a quill—Its important contents—Difficulty of complying with its instructions.

BEFORE entering into a detail of the operations carried on under the orders of Major-General Windham, for the defence of Cawnpore, when attacked by the mutineers of the Gwalior Contingent and other troops, it will be necessary to give a short account of the position of affairs, as they

Beginning of November.

existed on his taking the command, on the departure of the Commander-in-chief for the relief of Lucknow.

The critical position of the garrison at the latter place at the beginning of November, with the many women, children, and wounded in the Residency, together with the limited supply of provisions, rendered their relief a matter of vital and pressing necessity. They were isolated, and surrounded by at least 50,000 of the Oude mutineers and rebels. Every other consideration therefore gave way for the moment to the prosecution of this important scheme.

In order to insure success it became necessary to devote almost the whole of the available troops in that part of India for the purpose. The Commander-in-chief crossed the Ganges into Oude on the 9th of November, to assume command of the force engaged in this difficult operation, leaving Nov. 9. General Windham to guard Cawnpore. The garrison left for the latter consisted of the following troops:

		Total about
Infantry	{ 4 Companies of the 64th Regt, and small detachments of other Regts, }	.. 450
Seamen	.. ..	.. 47

These, with a few convalescent artillerymen, made up the strength to rather more than 500 men.*
It will be evident, by consulting a map of the

* A field battery of four guns was hastily organized, manned by a few European and Seikh gunners. The guns drawn by Commissariat bullocks.

country, that the safety of the position at Cawnpore now became a matter of the highest importance. It was to this point that the Commander-in-chief would return with the relieved garrison of Lucknow, and with all the women, children, and wounded. The intrenchment contained numerous guns, and a large proportion of ammunition, stores, provisions, &c. The preservation of the city also was of importance, as the inhabitants furnished supplies, saddlery, and other articles of use to the army.

The intrenchment at Cawnpore, on the right bank of the Ganges, had been commenced during the previous summer—(*vide* rough plan). It was an earthwork, and had been hurriedly constructed at a time of great pressure; was limited in extent, and unfinished; that part towards the canal being merely closed by a stockade, and, in fact, it could only be considered as an indifferent tête-de-pont, covering the bridge, which was thrown at that point over the Ganges. It is probable that its site was determined by the fact of that part of the river being the most convenient position for the bridge of boats, but one disadvantage was, that the ground round it, although flat, was encumbered with numerous houses, gardens, walls, &c., moreover, the old native city of Cawnpore, with its narrow streets, was only a few hundred yards distant; consequently an enemy might (if the city were not defended) approach even with artillery, under cover, to within easy musket-range of the works. It will therefore be seen that the intrenchment, although its safety was of such high importance, was one which it would be difficult to defend if seriously attacked. Some improvements were made to it by throwing up one or two outworks, but its principal defects could not altogether be remedied.

The instructions given to General Windham were to the following general effect.

His attention was called to the necessity of improving the defences.

He was directed to watch carefully the movements of the Gwalior force, which, it was supposed, would arrive at Calpee on the 9th of November. If this force should show a real intention of crossing the Jumna, the General was to use his discretion as to calling up the Futtepore garrison to reïnforce Cawnpore; but this was only to be as a last resource; and in that case an intermediate post, between Allahabad and Cawnpore, was to be formed at Sohunda, the terminus of the railway, by troops from Allahabad.

If positive information should be received of the movements of the Gwalior force, General Windham was to make as great a show as he could of the troops he might have at Cawnpore, by encamping them conspicuously outside, leaving a sufficient guard in the intrenchment, and looking well to his line of retreat.

General Windham was directed not to move out to attack, unless compelled to do so by circum-

DEFENCE OF CAWNPORE.

stances, to save the bombardment of the intrenchment.

For the present the garrison at Cawnpore was to consist of about 500 men. The detachments of British infantry, as they arrived up country, were to be sent into Oude, by wings of regiments, unless the General should be seriously threatened; but in the latter case he was to take the orders of the Commander-in-chief.

The General was to be allowed to retain the Madras Brigade on its arrival on the 10th of November, for a few days, until the intentions of the Gwalior Contingent became developed. The strength of the Brigade was about 450 native troops, with six * field guns.

In addition to the instructions, it was intimated to the General that it might be necessary (in the event of operations at Lucknow not proving successful) for him to come to the support of the Commander-in-chief.

General Windham, on assuming the command, at once took active measures to place the intrenchment in as complete a state of defence as possible. The works were extended and strengthened; the glacis was partially cleared; houses were blown down : 2000 coolies a day (including women and children) were employed in these duties, under the superintendence of Major M' Leod, Bengal En-

* Four of these were light six-pounders, manned by natives and drawn by bullocks, the other two were nine-pounders, horsed.

gineers. The number of guns mounted on the works was increased; but the deficiency was more in gunners than in guns.

These preparations were not uncalled for. No sooner had the Commander-in-chief left Cawnpore with the main body of the army, than the Gwalior Contingent, hitherto inactive at Calpee and Jaloun, began to show signs of life and to threaten an attack.

The Gwalior Contingent was known to be a well-disciplined dangerous body, complete in itself, with infantry, cavalry, and artillery; the men of the latter skilful, well drilled, and with a powerful siege train, their guns amounting in all to about 40 pieces, with 20,000 rounds of ammunition. Its movements had already excited anxiety; the influence of the Maharajah Scindiah had hitherto been successfully exerted in keeping this, his mutinous army, in a state of inaction. They had thus been prevented from swelling the ranks of the mutineers at Delhi, or from attacking Agra, but at the time now alluded to, they were at Jaloun and Calpee; the latter about 40 miles distant south-west of Cawnpore.

Cawnpore, with a whole rebel province in arms on one side; with a compact body of mutineers only a few marches off on the other, was, as will be seen, therefore, in a position of no ordinary peril; even its communications with the rear, by the Grand Trunk Road, were precarious and insecure; not many days had elapsed since a detachment, under the late Col. Powell of the 53rd Regiment, had met a force of the enemy near Bindkee in rear of Cawnpore.

About the middle of November the Gwalior Contingent,* although their movements were for some time uncertain and timid, gradually crossed the Jumna with their guns (both siege and field), and advanced parts of their force to Bognepore, thence on to Akbarpore, Shewlie, and Shirajpore. Their numbers at each place varied from day to day, and gradually increased, but on the 19th of November, were reported to be about as follows:— *Middle of November.*

Nov. 19.

At Calpee	3000 men	20 guns
Bognepore	1200 ,,	4 ,,
Akbarpore	2000 ,,	6 ,,
Shewlie	2000 ,,	4 ,,
Shirajpore	1000 ,,	4 ,,

and the remainder, with their reserves and treasure, at Jaloun.†

They thus formed a segment of a circle, as it were, round Cawnpore, closing the country and depriving that place of many supplies which had hitherto come in.

These preparations seemed to indicate an intention of attacking Cawnpore, but many officers of Indian experience thought differently, and were

---

* In speaking of the enemy as the "Gwalior Contingent," it is to be understood, that their chief force was composed of that body; but they were doubtless joined by many other mutineers, both before and after crossing the river Jumna.
† Vide outline plan of the country round Cawnpore.

of opinion that the enemy intended to avoid fighting, and were anxious gradually to cross our front and to get into Oude, where they would have swelled the numbers already in arms in that country. The Commander-in-chief himself, in his dispatch of the 2nd of December, concludes by saying, "All the previous reports had declared that there was but little chance of the Gwalior Contingent approaching Cawnpore." This was very possible, but General Windham, who, by means of spies, received constant intelligence of these movements of the enemy, although he was, to some extent, influenced by the opinions of others, still felt he must be prepared to consider these measures as the possible prelude of a concentrated attack upon his position. In fact, it was manifest that, if the enemy had any knowledge of military combinations, the very proper time for attacking Cawnpore from Calpee was, when the main body of the British army was withdrawn and engaged in a most serious operation 50 miles off in the opposite quarter.

Accordingly General Windham's exertions increased. He communicated constantly with the chief of the staff; he represented the insufficiency of his force to protect the city if attacked, and asked and obtained leave, about the 14th of November, to be allowed to detain detachments, instead of forwarding them to Lucknow;* by

---

* Previously to the 14th of November, all detachments arriving at

which means his garrison was gradually increased from 500, until on the 26th of November, when the first action was fought, he had about 1400 bayonets in the field, besides those left in the works (say in all about 1700 men*). He also wrote to the various officers and detachments who were on the march up the Trunk Road, desiring them to use all dispatch in joining him.

With the prospect of an increased force, General Windham's plans naturally became enlarged, and there seemed to be three courses open to him.

One, was to take out all his available troops (leaving sufficient to guard the intrenchment) and to attack and defeat the enemy in the open field, at one or more of their positions, and thus, if possible, beat them in detail before they could concentrate, returning of course at once to Cawnpore, when he had struck the blow. There might be a certain amount of risk in this, but it was doubtless the true strategy, if the strength of his force at all warranted certainty of success: to destroy an enemy in detail is manifestly one of the best chances for a small force against a vastly superior one. At the same time, in the present case, the primary consideration of course was the safety of the base of operations. On looking at the outline

---

Cawnpore had been sent on to Lucknow, and even as late as the 19th of November, a force of upwards of 300 men was sent to Alumbagh to escort ammunition, &c.

* This is exclusive of sick.

map, it will be perceived that Shewlie and Shirajpore, two positions of the enemy, were only about 15 miles from Cawnpore, whereas the main body of the mutineers was in the direction of Akbarpore and Bognepore, more than 25 miles off. To attack one or both of the former seemed to be very feasible, especially if it could be done by surprise; as in the event even of the main body of the enemy advancing, the General would have returned in time to defend his base. From Cawnpore runs the Ganges Canal, passing northwards, and a few miles distant between Shewlie and Shirajpore. The General conceived the idea, that if he were suddenly some night to transport about 1200 men along this canal, by means of its boats, and land them at daylight at a point on the road immediately between these two places, taking his field guns along the towing path, he would be able, with his troops quite fresh, to fall upon either of these two forces, as might appear from his latest intelligence most advisable, returning, as I have said, immediately after the battle.

For the prosecution of this idea he quietly assembled the boats near Cawnpore, and ascertained that they would readily contain the force required. The towing path was reconnoitred and found practicable for artillery: beyond Cawnpore there were no locks, and nothing therefore to cause delay. Even if the enemy should discover the plan during its progress, the troops could have landed at once without difficulty or confusion at

DEFENCE OF CAWNPORE. 11

any point. This plan was accordingly forwarded (about the 17th of November) to the Commander-in-chief, who was deeply engaged at the time in his operations at Lucknow, and authority was requested for its being executed. No direct reply was received, but the chief of the staff, in writing to Captain Bruce (the officer at the head of the intelligence department at Cawnpore), sent a message to General Windham, intimating that he should receive instructions.

Unfortunately after this answer (received 19th of November) the roads to Lucknow became closed: the communications interrupted by the enemy, and General Windham's letters after that date failed to reach the Commander-in-chief, nor did he for several days hear again from Lucknow.

Nov 19.

The second of the three courses open to General Windham was to take up some position with his main body outside the town, and in case of attack endeavour, if possible, to save it from pillage and destruction: he accordingly reconnoitred the environs with that view. Outside the town, and close to the walls and gardens which surround it, exist a number of high mounds, being old brick-kilns: these seemed to afford the desired means of defence. From their summits a good view was obtained over the surrounding country; by a little labour good cover could be found there for infantry; and even light field guns be mounted here and there in commanding positions. This scheme was also made known to head quarters.

The third course, and one that seemed contemplated by the original instructions, was to retire within the works, and hold them until the return of the army from Lucknow. The inevitable defects of the intrenchment have been already adverted to; besides, if the enemy were to attack, it became evident that, with heavy guns planted on the river's banks, they would be able to fire upon the bridge, the safety of which was so essential in every respect; and owing to the inequalities of the ground near the river, and the manner in which it was covered with houses and gardens, especially on the north side, there were some parts where the enemy could place their guns so as to batter the bridge, whilst they were themselves under shelter from the fire of the fort. Other points, too, were to be considered in abandoning the city, and merely confining the defence to the intrenchment; namely, that the army, which had gone to Lucknow, had left a certain amount of its baggage and stores in Bungalows, outside. There were also some houses which General Windham had prepared for the ladies, children, wounded, &c., shortly expected from Lucknow, all of which would, in that case, be given up to the enemy. The intrenchment was already crowded with stores and ammunition, &c. We may be considered to have arrived at about the 20th of November.

Nov. 20.

General Windham's anxieties now became very great on several accounts. The Gwalior Contingent were all round him in detached bodies, each

DEFENCE OF CAWNPORE.

within an easy march. In the mean time all communication from Lucknow suddenly ceased. The accounts up to the 19th of November had stated that access to the Residency had been gained after a succession of fights, and that the women and children might daily be expected. General Windham was aware, also, that there was some intention of attacking a very strong position of the enemy in the " Kaiser Bagh," at Lucknow. Suddenly, as has been said, all communication ceased. Each day he expected to see the advanced guard of the army returning from Lucknow with their precious convoy. Every hour he looked anxiously for letters, but none came; not even from Alumbagh. The road from Cawnpore to Alumbagh had hitherto been kept open by bodies of armed native police, stationed at various posts along the road; no troops being available for the purpose. On the 22nd of November intelligence was brought in, that a strong body of these police had been surprised and defeated, by the enemy, at the bridge of Bunnee, about 30 miles from Cawnpore on the Lucknow road. This was unfortunate, as it alarmed the men at the other stations, and rendered the chance of communication more remote. The General, however, feeling the importance of opening up the road (as possibly the army in Lucknow might be in difficulty), notwithstanding the small force at his command, immediately detached the Madras native regiment (already alluded to) with the two nine-pounder guns, to

Nov. 22.

proceed to Bunnee, with orders to hold the post, intrench, and communicate if possible with Alumbagh.

Nov. 23. On the 23rd of November a fresh cause of anxiety was added. A native arrived from Lucknow with a small note rolled up and concealed in a quill; one of the means by which the beleaguered garrison had frequently communicated with their friends outside. This note was dated 22nd of November, and was from a commissariat officer, with the Commander-in-chief's force, to a brother officer in the same department at Cawnpore. It stated, that the writer was desired to request that ten days' provisions for the whole force might at once be sent to Lucknow; that matters were getting complicated there. The note also desired that 50 rupees (£5) might be given to the bearer on its safe delivery, and added that the writer could give no opinion on military matters. This was a remarkable and an interesting document at that moment. It seemed singular that ten days' provisions should be asked for. It rather looked as if the Commander-in-chief's force were hemmed in, more especially as still no communication arrived from himself. Further, there was this great difficulty, that to send ten days' provisions would require an escort, which the General could ill spare, and would take away, moreover, almost all the transport of his small force, which would, in that case, be totally incapable of moving if required. Preparations, however, were made for sending the provisions as desired.

It will be clear, that whilst on the Lucknow side there was cause for anxiety, on the other there were the symptoms of a coming storm. On the one hand, General Windham knew not what difficulties might be encompassing the Commander-in-chief; on the other, he was momentarily threatened by an overwhelming attack. It was a moment of great anxiety, but fortunately the man was there whose spirit was equal to the occasion.

CHAPTER II.

24th of November—Mutineers from Oude cross the Ganges and join the Gwalior Contingent—General Windham advances to the canal—The reasons for this movement—Advance of the main body of the Gwalior Contingent—their leading division on the Pandoo Nuddy—The canal scheme abandoned—General Windham determines to fight the enemy on the Pandoo Nuddy—The reconnaissance—26th of November our troops advance—The order of battle—Stout resistance of the enemy—Their strong position captured—Three guns taken—General Windham retires to Cawnpore—receives a note from Lucknow.

Nov. 24. THE morning of the 24th arrived, and still no letter. The reports of the spies now gave notice that, instead of the Gwalior Contingent crossing into Oude, as many had supposed they intended, mutineers from Oude were stated as crossing at different Ghâts of the river with guns, and thus swelling the ranks of the Gwalior force. The crisis was evidently at hand, and immediate action became necessary.

General Windham, whose force was now almost daily augmenting, had hitherto had his main body encamped by the sanction of the Commander-in-chief outside the city, and close to the point of junction of the Delhi and Calpee roads. Expecting at any moment a message from Lucknow, and hoping it might bring authority for his carrying out the canal scheme, he decided, on the 24th, on advancing his camp close to the bridge by which

DEFENCE OF CAWNPORE. 17

the Calpee road crosses the canal. This might appear at first sight a rash move; but, in the first place, the canal served as a wide wet ditch along his whole front, and he kept a vigilant eye on the movements of the enemy on his flank, and patrolled all the roads incessantly, in case they should attempt to get round his rear; and he was thus placed in a position by which, although apparently showing an intention of advancing towards Calpee, he could in a few hours draw the canal boats to the spot, and carry out his intentions on Shewlie or Shirajpore.

Four companies of the 64th Regiment and a small force of artillery were left in the intrenchment. The 25th came, still no letter from Lucknow. The Gwalior Contingent, however, now began to assume the offensive, and to move rapidly to carry out their views. Accordingly, the spies reported the advance of their main body from Akbarpore to Suchonlee, and that their leading division was on the Pandoo river, only three miles from General Windham's camp. The canal scheme was now of course entirely abandoned. With the main body of the enemy so close, no move could now be made against the detached forces, more distant on the flank. But the General, feeling that to allow the enemy thus unopposed to approach so closely, was to give increased boldness to their movements, and knowing that with all armies there is an advantage with the attacking party (more especially in the case of Native Troops),

Nov. 26.

determined, boldly, to make a dash at their leading division, on the Pandoo Nuddy, if he should find them still bent on advancing; to strike as hard a blow as possible, and then at once to return, stand upon the defensive, and cover his base.

Nov. 26. Before daylight, accordingly, on the 26th of November, the troops were under arms, the baggage and camp equipage packed and sent to the rear, and the General, with his staff and ten men of the 9th Lancers, and the Sowars* at his disposal, went forward to reconnoitre. On approaching the Pandoo Nuddy, the enemy were found in considerable numbers, and the clouds of dust betrayed the movement of troops. They could be distinguished, dressed in their scarlet uniforms. Finding them in motion, orders were sent back for our force to advance. It amounted to about 1200 bayonets,† composed of the 34th Regiment, and parts of the 82nd and 88th Regiments, and 2nd battalion of Rifle Brigade with eight guns, four of which were nine-pounders (drawn by bullocks, manned by a few Royal Artillery and Bengal Gunners, and partly by Seikhs); the other four guns were light six-pounders, also drawn by bullocks, and manned by Madras Native Gunners.

The British troops advanced cheerfully to the attack. On approaching the enemy's position, the mutineers at once opened fire, and it was evident

---

* Sowars are native troopers.

† This total is exclusive of strong baggage guards, and also of a detachment which was left to guard the canal bridge.

DEFENCE OF CAWNPORE.

that their guns were of large calibre, and, as far as could be judged, there were about six in action. The battle, on the part of the British, began with the companies of the Rifle Brigade. These admirable troops at once advanced in skirmishing order on the right of the road. The country was a good deal encumbered with high standing corn, topes of trees, walls, &c. The Rifles were followed by the 88th Connaught Rangers, and the four light guns. The extreme right was covered by the Sowars. The 34th Regiment advanced at the same time on the left of the road; one wing in skirmishing order; the other in support with the four nine-pounder guns. The 82nd Regiment was held in reserve in column. Notwithstanding that our troops pressed eagerly forward to the attack, the enemy, who were about 3000 * in number, and strongly posted on the other side of the almost dry bed of the Pandoo Nuddy, held their ground for some time, and poured in several rounds of grape as we neared them. The extreme left of the line of skirmishers was charged by a body of the enemy's cavalry, but they were received by a volley from part of the 34th Regiment (which had formed square), and were driven away with loss. The troops then advanced with a rush, cheering as they went, passed rapidly across the bed of the river, and the position was won. The enemy fled precipitately, leaving two iron eight-inch How-

---

* 2500 infantry, 500 cavalry.

itzers, one six-pounder gun, and some ammunition waggons on the ground. They were followed for some distance through a small village, and their defeat completed by the fire of our artillery. General Windham, having halted for some time to rest his troops, withdrew, as he had intended, to a position in front of Cawnpore, taking his captured guns with him. He had observed, however, from a height beyond the village, that the main body of the enemy were not far distant, and their boldness in following up the British force as it retired showing plainly that, in spite of their defeat, they still had confidence in their overwhelming numbers and powerful artillery. The loss on our side was rather severe, considering the rapidity with which the attack had been made. It was as follows:

Killed	1 Officer	..	13 men.
Wounded	5 Officers	..	73 men.
	6		86
	Total casualties	..	92

The troops returned to Cawnpore in excellent spirits, after their successful attack, and General Windham at length received his long-desired letter from Lucknow. It was a short note from the chief of the staff, to the effect that all was well with the army, and that they were coming back at once to Cawnpore.

DEFENCE OF CAWNPORE. 21

CHAPTER III.

Morning of the 27th—Position of General Windham's troops—Difficulty of gaining information—At 10 A. M. the enemy commences a combined attack on the front and right flank—Disposition of our troops to meet them—Hard fighting in front—Powerful artillery of the mutineers—General Windham's force retires gradually to the brick-kilns—The enemy appear in the left front—The camp followers desert—The enemy get into the city in our rear—Retirement of our whole force into the Fort—Remarks on the operations.

In taking up a position on the afternoon of the 26th, it was General Windham's object, if possible, to cover the city and save it from pillage, and also to guard against any injury to the bridge over the Ganges. It was evident that, having regard to the probable movements of the enemy, neither of the two original places of encampment was now advisable. Both were too distant from the city, and left the flank exposed to danger. The camp was accordingly pitched on open ground, outside the town, across the Calpee road, immediately in front of the brick-kilns already alluded to.* There were several topes of trees near the camp, but it was in as open and free a space as could be found, considering the restricted choice which the circumstances allowed. The morrow might certainly find the troops engaged in a fresh contest, but

* See plan of battle of the 27th of Nov.

it was the general opinion (and it would seem a reasonable one) that the advance of the enemy would have been, to a certain degree, checked by the blow they had received on the 26th. On the morning of the 27th, before daylight, the troops were under arms as usual. The mutineers from Suchoulee were stated not to have crossed the canal in force, and their artillery was still on the other side of it. It was, however, difficult now to get accurate information. The spies feared to venture out: several during the previous days had returned horribly maimed, with their arms, ears, and noses cut off. There was no cavalry to perform outpost duty and bring in intelligence. The troops remained in camp ready to move as required. Two 24-pounder guns, manned by seamen of the "Shannon," and drawn by bullocks, were added to the artillery force. With an attack uncertain, and wishing to avoid creating unnecessary alarm among the inhabitants of the city, the General did not strike his camp. About ten o'clock A. M., as General Windham was reconnoitring from the top of a house on the outskirts of the village of Scesambow, a cannonade suddenly commenced on our right flank. Almost simultaneously a heavy fire of artillery was also heard in front. The enemy were evidently threatening on various points, and they at once commenced a serious attack on these two. The arrangements for meeting both are thus described in the despatch of the action.

" The heavy fighting in front, at the point of

DEFENCE OF CAWNPORE. 23

junction of the Calpee and Delhi roads, fell more especially upon the Rifle Brigade, ably commanded by Colonel Walpole, who was supported by the 88th Regiment and four guns (two nine-pounders, and two 24-pounders, Howitzers), under Captain D. S. Greene, Royal Artillery, and two 24-pounder guns manned by seamen of the 'Shannon,' under Lieutenant Hay, R. N., who was twice wounded."

* * * * * * * *

Again—

" The flank attack was well met and resisted, for a considerable time, by the 34th Regiment under Lieutenant Colonel Kelly, and the Madras Battery under Lieutenant Chamier, together with that part of the 82nd Regiment which was detached in this direction under Lieutenant Colonel Watson."

The remainder of the 82nd were placed near a wood on the right front, and thus completed the cordon of defence round the city, as far as the limited number of troops allowed. The position of these troops, and also of the enemy, is indicated in the accompanying rough plan of Cawnpore.

Conceiving that probably the flank attack would prove the more serious of the two (the fort being more accessible from that point), General Windham, in the first instance, proceeded there in person, sending orders to Colonel Walpole to hold on in front as long as possible. It will be perceived that two almost distinct battles were being fought at the same time. Our force at each point did not probably exceed 600 bayonets.

General Windham on his return to the front, after the lapse of about an hour, found matters there were serious. The attack of the enemy was vigorous, their fire of artillery rapid and well directed. Their guns were evidently far superior in number, and also in calibre. On our side the four nine-pounder guns were well worked; the two 24-pounders, which were on the road, kept up a heavy cannonade; the enemy, however, at length not only poured in a continued direct fire, but opened a flank one from guns placed along the Delhi road. One of the naval guns was turned in that direction to oppose them, but it was evident that, in spite of the resistance offered by the Rifles and Artillery, the fight was unequal; the ammunition began to fail; the bullock drivers began to desert; and it became necessary to fall back gradually; the naval guns, owing to their great weight, and the desertion of the bullock drivers, being with difficulty brought back. In order to reinforce his troops so severely engaged in front, General Windham withdrew for their support part of those who were less pressed on the flank. A body of the enemy, however, now appeared on the left front near the canal. Their numbers on all sides were evidently overwhelming.

To this new point of attack two companies of the 64th Regiment (withdrawn from the fort) were posted by the General himself. The fight had already lasted several hours, and betrayed no signs of abatement. The enemy gradually advanced their artillery, but showed no disposition to bring their infantry to close quarters. The British troops steadily fell back on the brick-kilns, covered by the Rifles, and the fire of the nine-pounder guns.

It seemed now that there was every probability that the position could be held. It was the very one originally intended by the General; his camp was close under his control, and the enemy dared not touch it. At an early period of the action, orders had been given to strike the camp, and send it with the baggage to the rear, but the camp followers, with their elephants, camels, &c., had fled, and the order could therefore only partially be obeyed. It was about 5 o'clock: the troops, sheltered by the brick-kilns, suffered but little from the enemy's fire.

General Windham, knowing that, in order to meet the severe engagement in his front, he had materially diminished the force originally detached to protect the flank, became now naturally very anxious to assure himself of the safety of the fort.

Part of the 88th Regiment had already been sent back to guard the Bithoor road, and on their passage through the town for that purpose, had encountered and bayonetted a certain number of the mutineers, who had probably found their way into the streets by making a circuit through the enclosures on the river's banks. A staff-officer was now sent back to ascertain and report on the state of affairs at the Fort, and to order up more ammunition. At length the General, finding that his position in front was tolerably secure, left General Dupuis, of the Royal Artillery, in command of the main body, with orders to hold on to the line of brick-kilns, whilst he himself galloped back to inspect personally the condition of matters at the intrenchment, and on the right flank.

He had not proceeded far before he met the staff-officer returning, who stated that the mutineers were in possession of the lower portion of the city; that they had just fired a volley in his face; and that they were attacking the Fort! Among the many trying moments of that trying day, this was probably the most critical. It so happened, that at this very time a detachment of the Rifle Brigade, which by forced marches had just arrived from Futtepore, were on the spot: General Windham, placing himself at their head, led them through the streets at a rapid pace, and the mutineers fled precipitately. Orders were in the mean time sent to General Dupuis to withdraw the whole force from the line of brick-kilns. This had become necessary, not from any pressure in front, but from the fact of the enemy having been found in the city a second time, it was clear that the main body of our troops was holding a position where they were liable to be cut off from their base. The enemy did not press our troops in their retreat to the intrenchment, which was made with perfect order, and not a man was lost in the operation.

Various criticisms have been passed upon the conduct of operations on this eventful day. It is not necessary to notice them here, as it is conceived that a plain statement of facts will be the best reply. It will be evident that the success of the enemy, although they fought well, especially with their artillery, was due rather to their immense superiority in numbers of men and guns, than to any other cause. General Windham considered it his duty to endeavour to save the city from pillage, but his numbers proved inadequate to cover so extended a front. No sooner were the enemy beaten back at one point, than they appeared in force at another. One or two minor errors were committed in the transmission of, and carrying out, his orders, but they did not probably materially affect the result.

The number of the enemy were stated in the Commander-in-chief's despatch of the 10th of December as amounting to about 25,000 men, and they had in all about 50 guns, of which 37 were eventually captured. The force under General Windham, including those in the Fort, amounted to about 1700 effective bayonets, and he had ten guns. It should also be borne in mind that his force, small as it was, was composed of detachments of various regiments, which had been rapidly pushed up the country, and had never hitherto acted together. He had no cavalry worth speaking of. His artillery, although he gave great credit to the officers and men who worked the guns, consisted of 10 pieces,* drawn by bullocks, manned by men of different nations, and therefore he laboured under great disadvantages in this respect, opposed to an enemy who were so numerous and efficient in this arm, and who had, moreover, several horsed batteries. Speaking of his retreat, his dispatch says, "In retiring within the intrenchments, I followed the general instructions issued to me by your Excellency, conveyed through the chief of the staff; namely, to preserve the safety of the bridge over the Ganges, and my communications with your force, so severely engaged in the important operation of the relief of Lucknow. As far as possible I *strictly* adhered to the defensive."

*   8 field guns.
2 24-pounder guns.
Total 10.

CHAPTER IV.

Night of the 27th—Proposed night attack, negatived—Arrangements for the 28th of November—The enemy again attack furiously both on the left and right fronts—A complete victory gained by our troops on the left—Two guns captured—Gallant conduct of the 64th Regiment on the right—their heavy loss—Obstinate fight of Brigadier Carthew—he retires at sunset—Return of the army from Lucknow—The enemy attack again on the 29th—The bridge over the Ganges struck with shot—The British force from Lucknow crosses the Ganges—Defeat of the Gwalior Contingent on the 6th of December—Conclusion.

THE night of the 27th was an anxious one, and was passed by the General and the superior officers chiefly in deliberation. The dispatch thus alludes to the subject, and also explains clearly the arrangements made for the following day.

"After falling back to the Fort, I assembled the superior officers on the evening of the 27th, and proposed a night attack, should I be able to receive reliable information as to where the enemy had assembled his artillery. As, however, I could obtain none (or, at all events, none that was satisfactory) I decided,

"Firstly, That on the following day, Colonel Walpole, Rifle Brigade, should have the defence of the advanced portion of the town on the left side of the canal, standing with your back to the Ganges. The details of the force upon this point were as follows: Nov. 28.

"Five companies of the Rifle Brigade under Lieutenant Colonel Woodford.

"Two companies of the 82nd Regiment under Lieutenant Colonel Watson.

"Four guns { two 9-pounders / two 24-pounders, Howitzers } under Captain Greene, R. A.

("Two of these guns were manned by Madras Gunners, and two by Seikhs.)

"Secondly, That Brigadier N. Wilson, with the 64th Regiment, was to hold the Fort and establish a strong picket at the Baptist Chapel on the extreme right.

"Thirdly, That Brigadier Carthew, with the 34th Regiment under Lieutenant Colonel Kelly, and four Madras guns, should hold the Bithoor Road.

"Fourthly, That, with the 88th Regiment under Lieutenant Colonel Maxwell, I should defend the portion of the town nearest the Ganges, on the left of the canal, and support Colonel Walpole if required." *

As had been anticipated, the enemy again attacked our position on the 28th. They evidently knew the value of time, and were anxious, if possible, to drive the Cawnpore force into the Ganges before succour could arrive from the army at Lucknow. Had they succeeded, the position of the Commander-in-chief, with the women, children, wounded, and treasure, would have been critical.

In the arrangements made by General Windham for the 28th, the great object was to keep the enemy as far as possible from the works, and to

* These dispositions will be rendered clear by consulting the plan of Cawnpore.

DEFENCE OF CAWNPORE. 31

prevent their flanking the bridge. It will be seen that the greater part of the troops, accordingly, were posted outside and considerably in advance. Two separate and very severe engagements were again fought, on this day, commencing about ten o'clock, A. M.; one on the left front, near the "Old Dragoon Lines;" the other on the right, beyond the Baptist Chapel. The former resulted in a complete victory, and is thus described in the despatch.

"On the left advance, Colonel Walpole, with the Rifles, supported by Captain Greene's battery, and part of the 82nd Regiment, achieved a complete victory over the enemy, and captured two 18-pounder guns. The glory of this well-contested fight belongs entirely to the above-named companies and artillery. It was owing to the gallantry of the men and officers, under the able leading of Colonel Walpole, and of my lamented relation, Lieutenant Colonel Woodford of the Rifle Brigade (who I deeply regret to say was killed), and of Lieutenant Colonel Watson, 82nd, and of Captain Greene, Royal Artillery, that this hard-contested fight was won and brought to so profitable an end. I had nothing to do with it, beyond sending them supports, and at the end of bringing some up myself."

The enemy were quite beaten off in this quarter. Their attack on the right, which was simultaneous with the other, was evidently made in immense force, and the ground afforded them great advantages. Soon after its commencement, a most determined and gallant attempt was made by part of the 64th Regiment to capture the enemy's guns. The dispatch relating to it says, "Brigadier Wilson thought proper, prompted by zeal for the service, to lead his regiment against four guns, placed in front of Brigadier Carthew. In this daring exploit, I regret to say, he lost his life, together with several valuable and able officers. Major F. Stirling, 64th Regiment, was killed in spiking one of the guns, as was also that fine gallant young man Captain R. C. M'Crea, 64th Regiment, who acted as Deputy Assistant Quarter Master General to the force here. Captain W. Morphey, 64th Regiment (the Brigade Major), also fell at the same time. Our numbers were not sufficient to enable us to carry off the guns."—After this attempt the enemy continued to press heavily in this quarter, and the position of the force under Brigadier Carthew, isolated and in advance of the Assembly Rooms, surrounded by walls and houses, behind which the enemy found shelter, was a difficult and a perilous one to maintain. Nevertheless, it was most gallantly held until nightfall: the 34th Regiment alone losing

3 officers killed,
7 officers wounded,
and 44 men killed and wounded.

There were also fifteen casualties among the Madras Gunners of the battery out of eighteen.

The total losses during the three days amounted to upwards of three hundred men.

DEFENCE OF CAWNPORE. 33

The troops, constantly fighting by day, and kept in alarm by feigned attacks at night, were a good deal exhausted. During the night of the 28th the enemy took complete possession of the town.

General Windham had already sent to inform the Commander-in-chief of the serious nature of the attack upon him, and on the evening of the 28th, the chief part of the force, from Lucknow, encamped on the other side of the Ganges. The independent command of General Windham then, of course, ceased. On the morning of the 29th the enemy, who, in spite of the presence of the force from Lucknow, still seemed to have entertained hopes of being able at all events to break the bridge across the Ganges, established heavy guns on the banks of the river, on the north side of the intrenchment, and struck the boats forming it three times with their shot. They were, however, held in check, and finally driven away, by a cross fire from guns of the Commander-in-chief's force, on the left bank, and from those in the Fort. The enemy also, under cover of the city, occasionally brought guns to bear upon the intrenchment, and the Hospital was struck repeatedly. During the 29th and 30th the whole force from Lucknow crossed over the bridge, and encamped near the " Old Dragoon lines."

The subsequent events are related in the despatches of the Commander-in-chief, dated 2nd and 10th of December, respectively. On the 6th of December an easy victory was obtained over

Nov. 29.

Nov. 30.

Dec. 6.

D

the Gwalior Contingent. With a British force consisting of several thousand infantry, with about 30 horsed field guns, and a fair proportion of cavalry, such a result was to be expected. The enemy on that occasion fled, and were pursued to the 15th mile-stone on the Calpee road, leaving their camp, 17 guns, and a large amount of ammunition in our hands. On the 8th of December, 15 more guns were captured by a force under Brigadier Hope Grant, without loss on our side.

The object with which this account has been drawn up, is to relate plainly the anxieties and responsibilities of General Windham's position; to explain also the reasons of his attacking the enemy in the open field on the first day; of his defence of the city on the second; and of his arrangements for protecting the intrenchment and bridge on the third.

If this account should tend to remove certain erroneous impressions which appear to have been formed on the subject, probably from a want of knowledge of details, the object in view will have been fully accomplished.

Return of ordnance captured from the Gwalior Contingent.

1857, 26th Nov.	By General Windham's force		3
— 28th Nov.	Do. Do.		2
— 6th Dec.	By the Commander-in-chief's force		17
— 8th Dec.	By Brigadier Grant's force		15

Total 37

APPENDIX.

OFFICIAL DESPATCHES.

I.

FROM MAJOR GENERAL C. A. WINDHAM, C. B. TO HIS EXCELLENCY, GENERAL SIR COLIN CAMPBELL, G. C. B., &c. &c. &c., COMMANDER-IN-CHIEF.

Cawnpore, 30th November, 1857.

SIR,

IN giving an account of the proceedings of the force under my command before Cawnpore during the operations of the 26th, 27th, 28th, and 29th instant, I trust your Excellency will excuse the hasty manner in which it is necessarily drawn up, owing to the constant demands upon me at the present moment.

Having received, through Captain H. Bruce, of the 5th Punjaub Cavalry, information of the movements of the Gwalior Contingent, but having received none whatever from your Excellency for several days from Lucknow, in answer to my letters to the chief of the staff, I was obliged to act for myself.

I therefore resolved to encamp my force on the canal, ready to strike at any portion of the advancing enemy that came within my reach, keeping at the same time my communications safe with Cawnpore.

Finding that the Contingent were determined to advance, I resolved to meet their first division on the Pandoo Nuddy. My force consisted of about 1200 bayonets, and eight guns, and 100 mounted Sowars. Having sent my camp equipage and baggage to the rear, I advanced to the attack in the following order :—

Four companies of the Rifle Brigade, under Colonel R. Walpole, followed by four companies of the 88th Connaught Rangers, under Lieutenant Colonel E. H. Maxwell, and four light six-pounder Madras guns, under Lieutenant Chamier; the whole under the command of Brigadier Carthew, of the Madras Native Infantry.

Following this force was the 34th Regiment, under Lieutenant Colonel R. Kelly, with four nine-pounder guns; the 82nd Regiment in reserve, with spare ammunition, &c.

I had given directions, in the event of the enemy being found directly in our front, and if the ground permitted, that Brigadier Carthew should occupy the ground to the left of the road, and that Lieutenant Colonel Kelly, with the 34th divided into wings, and supported by his artillery, should take the right. It so happened, however, that this order, on our coming into action, became exactly inverted by my directions in consequence of a sudden turn of the road. No confusion, however, was caused. The advance was made with a complete line of Skirmishers along the whole front, with supports on either side and a reserve in the centre.

The enemy, strongly posted on the other side of the dry bed of the Pandoo Nuddy, opened a heavy fire of artillery from siege and field guns; but such was the eagerness and courage of the troops, and so well were they led by their officers, that we carried the position with a rush, the men cheering as they went; and the village, more than half a mile in its rear, was rapidly cleared. The mutineers hastily took to flight, leaving in our possession two eight-inch iron Howitzers and one six-pounder gun.

In this fight my loss was not severe; but I regret very much that a very promising young officer, Captain H. H. Day, 88th Regiment, was killed.

Observing from a height on the other side of the village, that the enemy's main body was at hand, and that the one just defeated was their leading division, I at once decided on retiring to protect Cawnpore, my intrenchments, and the bridge over the Ganges. We accordingly fell back, followed, however, by the enemy up to the bridge over the canal.

On the morning of the 27th, the enemy commenced their attack, with an overwhelming force of heavy artillery. My position was in front of the city. I was threatened on all sides, and very seriously attacked on my front and right flank. The heavy fighting in front, at the point of junction of the Calpee and Delhi roads, fell more especially upon the Rifle Brigade, ably commanded by Colonel Walpole, who was supported by the 88th Regiment and four guns (two nine-pounders, two 24-pounder Howitzers), under Captain D. S. Greene, Royal Artillery, and two 24-pounder guns, manned by seamen of the *Shannon*, under Lieutenant Hay, R. N., who was twice wounded. Lieutenant Colonel John Adye, Royal Artillery, also afforded me marked assistance with these guns.

In spite of the heavy bombardment of the enemy, my troops resisted the attack for five hours, and still held the ground, until, on my proceeding personally to make sure of the safety of the Fort, I found, from the number of men bayonetted by the 88th Regiment, that the mutineers had fully penetrated the town; and having been told that they were then attacking the Fort, I directed Major-General

Dupuis, R. A. (who as my second-in-command I had left with the main body), to fall back the whole force into the Fort, with all our stores and guns, shortly before dark.

Owing to the flight of the camp-followers at the commencement of the action, notwithstanding the long time we held the ground, I regret to state, that in making this retrograde movement, I was unable to carry off all my camp equipage and some of the baggage. Had not an error occurred in the conveyance of an order issued by me, I am of opinion that I could have held my ground at all events until dark.

I must not omit, in this stage of the proceedings, to report that the flank attack was well met, and resisted, for a considerable time, by the 34th Regiment under Lieutenant Colonel Kelly, and the Madras Battery under Lieutenant Chamier, together with that part of the 82nd Regiment which was detached in this direction under Lieutenant Colonel D. Watson.

In retiring within the intrenchments, I followed the general instructions issued to me by your Excellency, conveyed through the chief of the staff, namely, to preserve the safety of the bridge over the Ganges, and my communications with your force, so severely engaged in the important operation of the relief of Lucknow, as far as possible. I strictly adhered to the defensive.

After falling back to the Fort, I assembled the superior officers on the evening of the 27th, and proposed a night attack, should I be able to receive reliable information as to where the enemy had assembled his artillery.

As, however, I could obtain none (or, at all events, none that was satisfactory), I decided—

Firstly.—That on the following day Colonel Walpole, Rifle Brigade, should have the defence of the advanced portion of the town on the left side of the Canal, standing with your back to the Ganges. The details of the force upon this point were as follows:—

Five companies Rifle Brigade, under Lieutenant Colonel C. Woodford.

Two companies of the 82nd Regiment, under Lieutenant Colonel Watson.

Four guns { Two nine-pounders } Under Captain
{ Two 24-pr Howitzers } Greene, R. A.

(Two of these guns were manned by Madras Gunners, and two by Seikhs.)

Secondly.—That Brigadier N. Wilson, with the 64th Regiment, was to hold the Fort and establish a strong picket at the Baptist Chapel on the extreme right.

Thirdly.—That Brigadier Carthew, with the 34th Regiment under Lieutenant Colonel Kelly, and four Madras guns, should hold the Bithoor road in advance of the Baptist Chapel, receiving support from the picket there if wanted.

Fourthly.—That, with the 88th Regiment under Lieutenant Colonel Maxwell, I should defend the portion of the town nearest the Ganges, on the left of the Canal, and support Colonel Walpole if required.

The fighting on the 28th was very severe. On the left advance, Colonel Walpole, with the Rifles, supported by Captain Greene's Battery, and part of the 82nd Regiment, achieved a complete victory over the enemy, and captured two 18-pounder guns.

The glory of this well-contested fight belongs entirely to the above-named companies and artillery.

It was owing to the gallantry of the men and officers under the able leading of Colonel Walpole, and of my lamented relation, Lieutenant Colonel Woodford, of the Rifle Brigade (who, I deeply regret to say, was killed), and of Lieutenant Colonel Watson, 82nd, and of Captain

Greene, R. A., that this hard-contested fight was won and brought to so profitable an end. I had nothing to do with it beyond sending them supports, and at the end of bringing some up myself.

I repeat that the credit is entirely due to the above-mentioned officers and men.

Brigadier Wilson thought proper, prompted by zeal for the service, to lead his regiment against four guns placed in front of Brigadier Carthew. In this daring exploit, I regret to say, he lost his life, together with several valuable and able officers. Major T. Stirling, 64th Regiment, was killed in spiking one of the guns, as was also that fine gallant young man, Captain R. C. M'Crea, 64th Regiment, who acted as Deputy Assistant Quarter Master General to the force here. Captain W. Morphey, 64th Regiment (the Brigade Major), also fell at the same time. Our numbers were not sufficient to enable us to carry off the guns.

Captain A. P. Bowlby, now the senior officer of the 64th Regiment, distinguished himself, as did also Captain H. F. Saunders, of the 70th Regiment, who was attached to the 64th, and is senior to Captain Bowlby, whose conduct he describes as most devoted and gallant; as was also that of the men of the regiment.

Brigadier Carthew, of the Madras Native Infantry, had a most severe and strong contest with the enemy from morning till night; but I regret to add, that he felt himself obliged to retire at dark.

During the night of the 28th instant, the enemy occupied the town, and on the morning of the 29th commenced bombarding my intrenchments with a few guns, and struck the bridge of boats several times.

The guns mounted in the Fort were superior in number to those of the enemy, and were well-manned, throughout the day, by the officers, non-commissioned officers, and men of the Royal Artillery, seamen of the *Shannon*, Madras and Bengal Gunners, and Seikhs.

The chief out-work was occupied by the Rifle Brigade, and in the course of the afternoon, by your Excellency's instructions, they were advanced, and gallantly drove the mutineers out of that portion of the city nearest to our works, under the command of Lieutenant Colonel Fyers, who was supported by Colonel Walpole.

Throughout the short period I have had the temporary command of this division, I have received, both in the field and elsewhere, the most important assistance from Captain H. Bruce, 5th Punjaub Cavalry. Without him I should have been at a great loss for reliable information, and although I am aware that your Excellency is not ignorant of his abilities, courage, and assiduity, I think it my duty to make this mention of his service to the country.

Pressed as I am by the operations now going forward, I am not able to specify the services of every individual who has assisted me, where all have behaved so well. I have no staff of my own, except Captain Roger Swire, of the 17th Foot, my aide-de-camp, who has behaved with his usual zeal and courage.

I therefore hope I may be allowed to thank, through your Excellency, the under-mentioned officers for the great services they have voluntarily rendered me during this trying time :—

Major General J. E. Dupuis, C. B., commanding Royal Artillery in India.
Lieutenant Colonel John Adye, C. B., Assistant Adjutant General, Royal Artillery. } Specially.
Lieutenant Colonel H. D. Harness, commanding Royal Engineers.
Major Norman M'Leod, Bengal Engineers.

Lieutenant Colonel John Simpson, 34th Regiment.
Senior Surgeon, R. C. Elliot, C. B., Royal Artillery.
Captain John Gordon, 82nd Regiment.
Captain Sarsfield Greene, Royal Artillery.
Captain Smyth, Bengal Artillery.

There are several other officers in addition, who I fortunately found detained here *en route* to join your Excellency's force, and I beg to submit their names also, viz.:—

Captain R. G. Brackenbury, 61st Regiment.
Lieutenant Arthur Henley, 52nd Light Infantry.
Lieutenant Valentine Ryan, 64th Regiment.
Captain Ellis Cunliffe, 1st Bengal Fusiliers.
Lieutenant E. H. Bugden, 82nd Regiment (to whom I gave the command of the 100 mounted Sowars).
Captain C. E. Mansfield, 33rd Regiment.
Lieutenant P. Scratchley, Royal Engineers.
Lieutenant W. C. Milne, 74th Bengal Native Infantry.

I beg to inform your Excellency that I have called for nominal returns of the killed and wounded, and I have also directed all officers commanding corps, regiments, and batteries, &c., to forward to me the names of any officers, non-commissioned officers, or soldiers, who may have especially distinguished themselves by gallantry in the field, which shall be forwarded to your Excellency without delay.

In conclusion, I hope I may be permitted to express my sincere thanks to all the regimental officers, non-commissioned officers, and men, for the zeal, gallantry, and courage with which they have carried out my orders during the four days of harassing actions, which have successively taken place in the defence of this important strategic centre of present operations.

I beg to forward the enclosed Despatch, which I have

received from Major General Dupuis; and I have called upon the various officers commanding corps, &c., to forward me the names of any officers they may wish to recommend, which I will send to your Excellency as soon as I receive them.

I have, &c.,
C. A. WINDHAM, MAJOR GENERAL.

II.

FROM HIS EXCELLENCY, GEN. SIR COLIN CAMPBELL, G. C. B., TO THE RIGHT HONOURABLE VISCOUNT CANNING, GOVERNOR GENERAL, CALCUTTA.

Head Quarters, Camp, Cawnpore, 2nd December, 1857.

MY LORD,

In accordance with the instructions of your Lordship, arrangements were finally made with Sir James Outram, that his division, made up to four thousand (4000) strong of all arms, should remain in position before Lucknow.

This position includes the post of Alumbagh, his standing camp, of which the front is fifteen hundred (1500) yards in rear of that post, and the bridge of Bunnee, which is held by four hundred (400) Madras Sepoys and two (2) guns.

On the 27th I marched with Brigadier General Grant's division, all the ladies and families who had been rescued from Lucknow, and the wounded of both forces, making in all about two thousand (2000) people, whom it was necessary to carry, and encamped the evening of that day a little beyond Bunnee bridge.

The long train did not reach completely and file into camp until after midnight.

When we arrived at Bunnee, we were surprised to hear very heavy firing in the direction of Cawnpore. No news had reached me from that place for several days; but it appeared necessary, whatever the inconvenience, to press forward as quickly as possible.

The march accordingly recommenced at nine A. M. the next morning, and shortly afterwards I received two or three notes in succession,—*first*, announcing that Cawnpore had been attacked; *secondly*, that General Windham was hard pressed; and *thirdly*, that he had been obliged to fall back from outside the city into his intrenchment.

The force was accordingly pressed forward, convoy and all, and was encamped within three miles of the Ganges, about three hours after dark, the rear-guard coming in with the end of the train some twenty-four hours afterwards.

I preceded the column of march by two or three hours, and reached the intrenchment at dusk, where I learnt the true state of affairs.

The retreat of the previous day had been effected with the loss of a certain amount of camp equipage, and shortly after my arrival, it was reported to me that Brigadier Carthew had retreated from a very important outpost.

All this appeared disastrous enough, and the next day the city was found to be in possession of the enemy at all points.

It had now become necessary to proceed with the utmost caution to secure the bridge.

All the heavy guns attached to General Grant's division, under Captain Peel, R. N., and Captain Travers, R. A., were placed in position on the left bank of the Ganges, and directed to open fire and keep down the fire of the enemy on the bridge.

This was done very effectually, while Brigadier Hope's Brigade, with some field artillery and cavalry, was ordered to cross the bridge, and take position near the Old Dragoon Lines.

A cross fire was at the same time kept up from the intrenchment, to cover the march of the troops.

When darkness began to draw on the Artillery Parks, the wounded and the families were ordered to file over the bridge; and it was not till six o'clock, P. M., the day of the 30th, that the last cart had cleared the bridge.

The passage of the force, with its encumbrances, over the Ganges, had occupied thirty hours.

The camp now stretches from the dragoon lines in a half circle round the position occupied by the late General Sir Hugh Wheeler, the foot artillery lines being occupied by the wounded and the families.

A desultory fire has been kept up by the enemy on the intrenchment and the front of the camp since this position was taken up, and I am obliged to submit to the hostile occupation of Cawnpore, until the actual despatch of all my encumbrances towards Allahabad has been effected.

However disagreeable this may be, and although it may tend to give confidence to the enemy, it is precisely one of those cases in which no risk must be run.

I trust, when the time has arrived for me to act with due regard to these considerations, to see the speedy evacuation of his present position by the enemy.

In the mean time, the position taken up by Brigadier General Grant's division, under my immediate orders, has restored the communications with Futtehpore and Allahabad, as had been anticipated. The detachments moving along the road from these two places, have been ordered to continue their march accordingly.

Major General Windham's Despatch, relating to the operations conducted under his command, is enclosed.

In forwarding that document, I have only to remark that the complaint made by him in the second paragraph, of not receiving instructions from me, is explained by the fact of the letters he sent announcing the approach of the Gwalior force not having come to hand.

The first notice I had of his embarrassment was the distant sound of cannonade, as above described.

All the previous reports had declared that there was but little chance of the Gwalior Contingent approaching Cawnpore.

I have, &c.,

C. CAMPBELL, GENERAL.

Commander-in-chief.

P. S.—Annexed is a return of casualties from the 29th ultimo to this date.

III.

FROM GENERAL SIR COLIN CAMPBELL, G.C.B., TO THE RIGHT
HONOURABLE VISCOUNT CANNING, GOVERNOR GENERAL,
CALCUTTA.

Head Quarters, Camp, Cawnpore, the 10th December, 1857.

My Lord,

I have the honour to report to your Lordship, that late on the night of the 3rd instant, the convoy, which had given me so much anxiety, including the families and half of the wounded, was finally despatched, and on the 4th and 5th the last arrangements were made for consigning the remainder of the wounded in places of safety, while a portion of the troops was withdrawn from the intrenchments to join the camp.

On the afternoon of the 5th, about three P. M., the enemy attacked our left pickets with artillery, and showed infantry round our left flank.

A desultory fire was also begun on our pickets in the General Gung, which is an old bazaar of very considerable extent along the canal, in front of the line occupied by the camp.

These advanced positions had been held, since our arrival, by Brigadier Greathed's Brigade with great firmness, the Brigadier having displayed his usual judgment in their arrangement and support. On two or three occasions he had been supported by Captain Peel's heavy guns and Captain Bourchier's field battery, when the artillery of the enemy had annoyed him and the general front of the camp.

After two hours of cannonading, the enemy retired on the afternoon in question.

Arrangements were then made for a general attack on him the next day.

His left occupied the old Cantonment, from which General Windham's post had been principally assailed. His centre was in the city of Cawnpore, and lined the houses and bazaars overhanging the canal, which separated it from Brigadier Greathed's position, the principal streets having been afterwards discovered to be barricaded.

His right stretched some way beyond the angle formed by the Grand Trunk road and the canal, two miles in rear of which the camp of the Gwalior Contingent was pitched, and so covered the Calpee road. This was the line of retreat of that body.

In short, the canal, along which were placed his centre and right, was the main feature of his position, and could only be passed in the latter direction by two bridges.

It appeared to me, if his right were vigorously attacked, that it would be driven from its position without assistance coming from other parts of his line, the wall of the town which gave cover to our attacking columns on our right being an effective obstacle to the movement of any portion of his troops from his left to right.

Thus the possibility became apparent of attacking his division in detail.

From intelligence received before and after the action, there seems to be little doubt that in consequence of the arrival of four regiments from Oude, and the gathering of various mutinous corps which had suffered in previous actions, as well as the assemblage of all the Nana's followers, the strength of the enemy now amounted to about 25,000 men, with all the guns belonging to the Contingent, some thirty-six (36) in number, together with a few guns belonging to the Nana.

Orders were given to General Windham, on the morning of the 6th, to open a heavy bombardment at nine A. M., from the intrenchment in the old cantonment, and so induce the belief in the enemy that the attack was coming from the General's position.

The camp was struck early, and all the baggage driven to the river side under a guard, to avoid the slightest risk of accident.

Brigadier Greathed, reïnforced by the 64th Regiment, was desired to hold the same ground opposite the centre of the enemy, which he had been occupying for some days past, as above-mentioned, and at 11 A. M. the rest of the force, as per margin, was drawn up in contiguous columns in rear of some old cavalry lines, and effectually masked from the observation of the enemy.

Brigadier Greathed's Brigade.
H. M.'s 8th Foot.
H. M.'s 64th Foot.
2nd Punjaub Infantry.

Artillery Brigade.
Two Troops Horse Artillery.
Three Light Field Batteries.
Guns of the Naval Brigade.
Heavy Field Battery Royal Artillery.

Cavalry Brigade.
H. M.'s 9th Lancers.
Detachments 1st, 2nd, and 5th Punjaub Cavalry, and Hodson's Horse.

4th Infantry Brigade.
H. M.'s 53rd Regiment.
H. M.'s 42nd and 93rd Highlanders.
4th Punjaub Rifles.

5th Infantry Brigade.
H. M.'s 23rd Fusiliers.
H. M.'s 32nd Regiment.
H. M.'s 82nd Regiment.

6th Infantry Brigade.
2nd and 3rd Battalion Rifle Brigade.
Detachment H. M.'s 38th Foot.

Engineer Brigade.
Royal Engineers and Detachments Bengal and Punjaub.
Sappers and Miners attached to the various Brigades of Infantry.

The cannonade from the intrenchment having become slack at this time, the moment had arrived for the attack to commence.

The cavalry and horse artillery, having been sent to make a detour on the left, and cross the canal by a bridge a mile and a half further up, and threaten the enemy's rear.

The infantry deployed in parallel lines fronting the canal.

Brigadier Hope's brigade was in advance in one line, Brigadier Inglis' brigade being in rear of Brigadier Hope.

At the same time Brigadier Walpole, assisted by Captain Smith's field battery, Royal Artillery, was directed to pass the bridge immediately to the left of Brigadier Greathed's position, and to drive the enemy from the brick-kilns, keeping the wall of the city for his guide.

The whole attack then proceeded, the enemy quickly responding from his proper right to the fire of our heavy and field artillery.

Good use was made of these guns by Captain Peel, C. B., R. N., and the artillery officers under Major General Dupuis, C. B., R. A., Brigadier Crawford, R. A., and Major Turner, B. A.

The Seikhs of the 4th Punjaub Infantry, thrown into skirmishing order, supported by H. M.'s 53rd Foot, attacked the enemy in some old mounds and brick-kilns to our left with great vigour.

The advance then continued with rapidity along the whole line, and I had the satisfaction of observing in the distance that Brigadier Walpole was making equal progress on the right.

The canal bridge was quickly passed, Captain Peel leading over it with a heavy gun, accompanied by a soldier of H. M.'s 53rd, named Hannaford.

The troops which had gathered together, resuming their line of formation with great rapidity on either side as soon as it was crossed, and continuing to drive the enemy at all points, his camp being reached and taken at one P. M., and his rout being complete along the Calpee road.

I must here draw attention to the manner in which the heavy 24-pounder guns were impelled and managed by Captain Peel and his gallant sailors.

Through the extraordinary energy and good-will with which the latter have worked, their guns have been constantly in advance throughout our late operations, from the relief of Lucknow till now, as if they were light field pieces, and the service rendered by them in clearing our front has been incalculable. On this occasion there was the sight beheld of 24-pounder guns advancing with the first line of skirmishers.

Without losing any time, the pursuit with cavalry, infantry, and light artillery has pressed with the greatest eagerness to the fourteenth milestone on the Calpee road, and I have reason to believe that every gun and cart of ammunition, which had been in that part of the enemy's position which had been attacked, now fell into our possession.

I had the satisfaction of accompanying the troops engaged in the pursuit, and of being able to bear witness to their strenuous endeavours to make the most of the success which had been achieved.

When I passed the camp and went forward on the Calpee road, Major-General Mansfield was desired by me to make arrangements for the attack of the position called the Subadar's Tank, which extended round the left rear of the enemy's position in the old Cantonments. As this operation was a separate one, I beg to enclose, for your Lordship's consideration, the Major-General's own Narrative.

The troops having returned from the pursuit at midnight on the 6th, and their baggage having reached them on the afternoon of the next day, Brigadier General Grant was detached in pursuit on the 8th with the cavalry, some light artillery, and a brigade of infantry, with orders to destroy public buildings belonging to the Nana Sahib at Bithoor, and to press on to Serai Ghât, twenty-five miles from hence, if he had good tidings of the retreating enemy. This duty was admirably performed by the Brigadier General, and he caught the enemy when he was about to cross the river with his remaining guns.

The Brigadier General attacked him with great vigour, and by the excellent disposition he made of his force, succeeded in taking every gun the enemy possessed, without losing a single man. I have the pleasure to enclose the Brigadier General's report for your Lordship's perusal.

It now remains for me to bring to your Lordship's notice the officers who have distinguished themselves during the series of operations which have occurred under my own eyes, since this field force left the neighbourhood of Lucknow.

I have a particular pleasure in again bringing to your Lordship's notice the zeal and great ability with which Major General W. R. Mansfield, chief of the staff, has conducted the very important duties of his high position, and of my obligations to him for the most valuable assistance he has afforded me during the whole of the recent operations. I desire also to call your Lordship's attention to the able and distinguished manner in which he conducted the troops placed under his orders, after the enemy's centre had been divided, to the attack of their strong position at the Subadar's Tank, and to recommend to your Lordship's favourable consideration the names of the officers who assisted him.

I have to thank Brigadier General Hope Grant, C. B., very particularly for the admirable manner in which he has conducted the duties of the force, and more particularly for his exertions on the 6th December, and the capital operations he performed on the 8th and 9th. The Brigadier General speaks in the highest terms of his divisional and personal staff, viz., Captain W. Hamilton, Deputy Assistant Adjutant General; Lieutenant F. S. Roberts, Deputy Assistant Quarter Master General; Captain the Honourable A. H. Anson, Aide-de-camp; Lieutenant C. W. Havelock, extra Aide-de-camp; and Captain H. M. Wilson, Deputy Judge Advocate General.

I have the greatest satisfaction in bringing to your Lordship's notice, Brigadiers Greathed, the Honourable A. Hope, Walpole, and Inglis. These officers have all exerted themselves to the utmost, and have fully justified my expectations. They desire to record their obligations to the officers commanding corps in their respective brigades and to their brigade staff, as follows:—

Captain Hinde, Her Majesty's 8th Regiment; Lieutenant Colonel Wells, Her Majesty's 23rd Fusiliers; Major Lowe, commanding Her Majesty's 32nd Regiment; Lieutenant Colonel Kelly, Her Majesty's 38th Regiment; Lieutenant Colonel Thorold, Her Majesty's 42nd Highlanders; Colonel Faber, Her Majesty's 53rd Regiment; Major Bingham, Her Majesty's 64th Regiment; Lieutenant Colonel Hale, Her Majesty's 82nd Regiment; Lieutenant Colonel Leith Hay, Her Majesty's 93rd Highlanders; Lieutenant Colonel Horsford, 3rd Battalion Rifle Brigade; Lieutenant Colonel Fyers, 2nd Battalion Rifle Brigade; Captain Green, commanding 2nd Punjaub Infantry; Lieutenant W. C. L. Ryves, commanding 4th Punjaub Rifles; Captain J. M. Bannatyne, Brigade Major, 3rd Brigade; Captain J. H. Cox, Brigade Major, 4th Brigade; Captain Lightfoot, Brigade Major, 5th Brigade; Lieutenant C. A. Barwell, Brigade Major, 6th Brigade.

Owing to his knowledge of the ground I requested Major General Windham to remain in command of the intrenchment, the fire of which was a very important feature in the operations of the 6th December, although I felt and explained to General Windham that it was a command hardly worthy of an officer of his rank. He gave me every satisfaction, and I have to thank him accordingly.

I must particularly notice the exertions of Captain H. W. Norman, Assistant Adjutant General of the Army; of Captain Herbert Bruce, Deputy Quarter Master General; and of Captain J. H. Smyth, Bengal Artillery, the latter of whom had been requested by me to take command of the artillery in the intrenchment as a special duty.

Captain Smyth has rendered other great and valuable services since he left Calcutta, of which I have not had an opportunity before of recording my approval.

I desire also to bring to your Lordship's favourable notice, the officers on the general staff or belonging to the personal staff of myself or Major General Mansfield, viz. Captain H. R. Garden, Assistant Quarter Master General; Lieutenant G. Allgood, and Captain T. A. Carey, Deputy Assistants Quarter Master General; Captain G. C. Hatch, Deputy Judge Advocate General of the army; Captain Sir David Baird, Bart., my first Aide-de-camp; Captain J. Metcalfe, Interpreter; Lieutenant W. O. Lennox, Royal Engineers; Captain W. Rudham, Acting Assistant and Adjutant General, Her Majesty's forces; Lieutenant Hope Johnstone, Deputy Assistant Adjutant General to the chief of the staff; Lieutenant F. M. Alison, and Captain Forster, my Aides-de-camp; and Captain Mansfield and Lieutenant D. M. Murray, Aide-de-camp, and extra Aide-de-camp to the chief of the staff.

To the crew of H. M. S. *Shannon*, and to the Royal and Bengal Artillery, my thanks are alike due; but more particularly to Captain Peel, C. B., Royal Navy; to Brigadier

Crawford, Royal Artillery; and to Major Turner, Bengal Horse Artillery. I cannot refrain from again drawing your Lordship's most marked attention to the very distinguished merits of the last-named (Major Turner).

As is always the case in the three services, the batteries and troops were manœuvred with remarkable dexterity.

Captain Peel has brought to my favourable notice Lieutenant Vaughan, Royal Navy, and I should much wish that this recommendation may be known at the Admiralty; and Brigadier Crawford has expressed his obligations to his Brigade Major, Captain H. L. G. Bruce, Bengal Artillery, and has mentioned with marked distinction all the officers holding commands, viz. Captain Travers, commanding Royal Artillery; Captains Remmington and Blunt, commanding troops of Bengal Horse Artillery; Captains Middleton and Smith, Royal Artillery; and Captain Bourchier, Bengal Artillery, commanding light field batteries; Captain Longden, Royal Artillery, commanding a heavy battery; and Lieutenant Bridge, commanding two guns, Madras Horse Artillery.

Major General Dupuis, C. B., Royal Artillery, commanded the artillery during the action, in consequence of his accidental presence in camp, and I beg to thank him for his exertions as well as those of his staff, viz. Lieutenant Colonel Adye, C. B., R. A., Assistant Adjutant General, and Captain Greene, R. A., Aide-de-camp.

Colonel Harness, Royal Engineers, was also present in the same manner, and accompanied me throughout the action.

General Grant has also brought to my notice the distinguished conduct of Brigadier Little, commanding the Cavalry, as also of officers commanding corps in that brigade and its staff officers, viz.:—

Major Ouvry, 9th Lancers; Lieutenant Watson, 1st

Punjaub Cavalry; Lieutenant Probyn, 2nd Punjaub Cavalry; Lieutenant Younghusband, 5th Punjaub Cavalry; Lieutenant H. Gough, Hodson's Horse; and Captain H. A. Sarel, Major of Brigade.

During the pursuit of the 6th, and the operation of the 9th, the cavalry maintained that high character for dash and perseverance which have distinguished them since they took the field in the numerous engagements of their long campaign.

I desire also to mention Major Payne, of the 53rd Regiment, whom I saw performing very valuable service during the first advance on the 6th instant.

I must not allow this opportunity to pass without bearing my testimony to the unwearied zeal and assiduity of the Superintending Surgeon, Doctor J. C. Brown, Bengal Artillery, which have never flagged for an instant, and have been of the greatest use to the force in the field, from the time the troops first took the field before going to Delhi.

I beg to recommend him most particularly to your Lordship's favourable consideration.

Annexed are returns of killed and wounded, and of captured ordnance, as well as a sketch of the ground.

I have, &c.,

C. CAMPBELL, GENERAL,

Commander in-chief.

IV.

The Right Honourable the Governor General in Council has received the accompanying despatch from his Excellency the Commander-in-chief, and hastens to give publicity to it.

It supplies an omission in a previous despatch from his Excellency, which was printed in the *Gazette Extraordinary* of the 24th instant.

Major General Windham's reputation as a leader of conspicuous bravery and coolness, and the reputation of the gallant force which he commanded, will have lost nothing from an accidental omission, such as General Sir Colin Campbell has occasion to regret.

But the Governor General in Council will not fail to bring to the notice of the government in England the opinion formed by his Excellency of the difficulties against which Major General Windham, with the officers and men under his orders, had to contend.

TO THE RIGHT HONOURABLE THE GOVERNOR GENERAL.

Head Quarters, Camp, near Cawnpore,
the 20th of December, 1857.

My Lord,

I have the honour to bring to your Lordship's notice an omission, which I have to regret, in my despatch of the 2nd December, and I beg to be allowed now to repair it.

I desire to make my acknowledgment of the great difficulties in which Major General Windham, C. B., was placed during the operations he describes in his despatch, and to recommend him and the officers, whom he notices as having rendered him assistance, to your Lordship's protection and good offices.

I may mention, in conclusion, that Major General Windham is ignorant of the contents of my despatch of 2nd December, and that I am prompted to take this step solely as a matter of justice to the Major General and the other officers concerned.

I have the honour to be,

My Lords,

With the greatest respect,

Your Lordship's

Most obedient humble servant,

C. CAMPBELL, GENERAL,

Commander-in-chief.

www.ingramcontent.com/pod-product-compliance
Lightning Source LLC
Chambersburg PA
CBHW032011080426
42735CB00007B/571